This book belongs to:

The Letterlanders

Annie Apple	Bouncy Ben	Clever Cat	Dippy Duck	Eddy Elephant	Fireman Fred	Golden Girl

    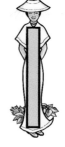 

Hairy Hat Man	Impy Ink	Jumping Jim	Kicking King	Lucy Lamp Lady	Munching Mike

Naughty Nick	Oscar Orange	Poor Peter	Quarrelsome Queen	Robber Red	Sammy Snake	Ticking Tess

Uppy Umbrella	Vase of Violets	Wicked Water Witch	Max and Maxine	Yellow Yo-yo Man	Zig Zag Zebra

   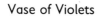 

Letterland ®

Alphabet Adventures

Published by Collins Educational
An imprint of HarperCollins*Publishers* Ltd
77-85 Fulham Palace Road
London W6 8JB

www.**Collins**Education.com
On-line support for schools and colleges

© Lyn Wendon 2000

First published in hardback 1996
This paperback edition published 2000
Reprinted 10 9 8 7 6 5 4 3

ISBN 0 00 303474 7

LETTERLAND® is a registered trademark of Lyn Wendon.

Jane Launchbury asserts the moral right to be identified as the author of this work.

British Library Cataloguing in Publication Data
A catalogue record for this book is available from the British Library.

Written and illustrated by Jane Launchbury
Colourist: Dulce Tobin
Designer: Mike Sturley
Consultant: Lyn Wendon, originator of Letterland

Printed by
Printing Express, Hong Kong

www.**fire**and**water**.com
Visit the book lover's website

Letterland ®

Alphabet Adventures

**Written and illustrated
by Jane Launchbury**

Collins

An imprint of HarperCollins*Publishers*

At the seaside

'A day by the sea is good for me,'
Says Sammy Snake sleepily.
All his Letterland friends agree.
How many of them can you see?

Off to the fair!

Let's all go to the Letterland fair!
But how shall we get from here to there?
Ticking Tess will take the train,
Poor Peter prefers to go by plane.
Robber Red races on roller skates.
Can you find his Letterland mates?

4

Let's go shopping!

Sammy Snake is selling sweets,
Ticking Tess is buying treats.
Oscar Orange has lost his brother,
Munching Mike stays close to his mother.
While you search for all the rest,
Which of the shops do you like best?

Jungle adventure

High up in the jungle trees
Jumping Jim says 'Help me, please.
Help me find my Letterland chums
Before the hungry tiger comes!'

At the airport

Jumping Jim is shouting 'Hooray!'
He's just off on a holiday.
Some of his friends are coming back.
But what is that in Robber Red's sack?

Duty-Free Shop

V.A.T.

Baggage Reclaim

Red channel

customs
officers
only

Customs

11

Down by the river

Lamp Lady Lucy is on her way
To join us on this sunny day.
What do you think she'd like to eat
As a special picnic treat?

Fun on the farm

Down on the farm there's Bouncy Ben.
He's busy feeding a noisy hen.
Behind the barn, poor Ticking Tess
Is cleaning up a nasty mess!
Most of their friends are busy too.
The bird can see them all, can you?

15

Classroom chaos

Who can it be in the Letterland school
That's broken one important rule?
Never let a rhino loose
Without a very good excuse!

In hospital

Oh dear, dear! Poor Fireman Fred!
He fell downstairs and bumped his head.
Sammy Snake ate too much cake
And now he's got a tummy ache!
Look at the picture. Can you say
What's going on in the hospital today?

Playing in the park

Poor Peter Puppy is happy today.
He's in the park and he's ready to play.
Most of his friends are having fun,
But can you spot the unlucky one?

Wishing Well

At the zoo

Can you hear the hullabaloo
Coming from the Letterland Zoo?
Join us there to see what's new...
A lovely baby kangaroo!

Hot House

It's party time!

Quarrelsome Queen would like to invite
You all to her fancy dress party tonight.
Now she is wondering who is who.
Search for every little clue!

Quarrelsome Queen's questions

Can you find a picture of ...

1   Annie Apple covered in ants?

2   Bouncy Ben being a butterfly?

3   Clever Cat looking cross?

4   Dippy Duck in a drawer?

5   Eddy Elephant and eleven eggs?

6   Fireman Fred holding a flag?

7   Golden Girl holding a bunch of green grapes?

8   Hairy Hat Man without his hat on?

9   Impy Ink and six big insects?

10 Jumping Jim doing a jigsaw?

11 Kicking King with a bunch of keys?

12 Lucy Lamp Lady looking for a lost lamb?

13 Munching Mike in a motorboat?

14 Naughty Nick being a nice nurse?

15 Oscar Orange with an orang-utan?

16 Poor Peter eating a piece of pork pie?

17 Quarrelsome Queen quarrelling with a squirrel?

18 Robber Red rowing on a river?

19 Sammy Snake and a scarecrow?

20 Ticking Tess talking to a tiger?

21 Uppy Umbrella looking unhappy?

22 Vase of Violets on a video camera?

23 Wicked Water Witch wading in the water?

24 Max and Maxine in a taxi?

25 Yellow Yo-yo Man yawning?

26 Zig Zag Zebra zipping up a bag?

The Letterlanders

| Annie Apple | Bouncy Ben | Clever Cat | Dippy Duck | Eddy Elephant | Fireman Fred | Golden Girl |

| Hairy Hat Man | Impy Ink | Jumping Jim | Kicking King | Lucy Lamp Lady | Munching Mike |

| Naughty Nick | Oscar Orange | Poor Peter | Quarrelsome Queen | Robber Red | Sammy Snake | Ticking Tess |

| Uppy Umbrella | Vase of Violets | Wicked Water Witch | Max and Maxine | Yellow Yo-yo Man | Zig Zag Zebra |

OTHER LETTERLAND TITLES AVAILABLE IN PAPERBACK...

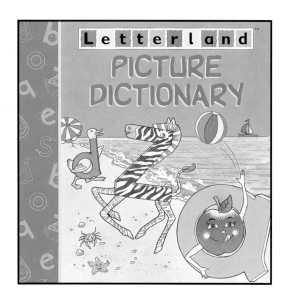

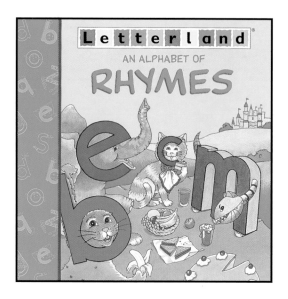

For further information on Letterland products call 0141-306-3100
0141-306-3391

The Letterland alphabet is the basis of the well-known Letterland system for the teaching of reading used in the majority of English primary schools.